RAISE YOUR OWN MONARCH BUTTERFLIES

EVERYTHING YOU NEED TO KNOW:

FEEDING, HOUSING, HABITANT, HEALTH AND DIET,

PREDATOR AND LIFE CYCLE, MIGRATION

Annie Carrol

Raise Your Own Monarch Butterflies

COPYRIGHT

Copyright © 2021 by **Annie Carrol**: All rights reserved. This book or any portion thereof may not be reproduced or used in any manner whatsoever without the express written permission of the author except for the use of brief quotations in a book review.

Table of Contents

INTRODUCTION

CHAPTER ONE

WHY SHOULD WE RAISE BUTTERFLIES, MONARCH BUTTERFLIES, AND OTHER SPECIES?

CHAPTER TWO

WHERE TO LOOK FOR CATERPILLARS

CHAPTER THREE

COLLECTION OF CATERPILLARS

CHAPTER FOUR

MAKE A CATERPILLAR HOUSING

CHAPTER FIVE

WHAT DO CATERPILLARS EAT?

CHAPTER SIX

WAIT RIGHT NOW

CHAPTER SEVEN

RAISING BUTTERFLY CATERPILLAR INDOORS

CHAPTER EIGHT

BUILDING A BUTTERFLY GARDEN

CHAPTER NINE

CHOOSING THE IDEAL BUTTERFLY HOUSE

CHAPTER TEN

IS A BUTTERFLY AN INSECT?

CHAPTER ELEVEN

BUTTERFLY FUN FACTS

CONCLUSION

Raise Your Own Monarch Butterflies

INTRODUCTION

My husband gave up cutting the grass on the steep slope that runs the length of our property about a decade ago. Instead, we eradicated the grass and replaced it with natural grassland. Other flowers and plants have since blown in on the breeze or been carried in by pollinators. Milkweed is one of them, and it is the primary food source for monarch caterpillars.

Every year, my children and I excitedly await the arrival of caterpillars on our milkweed. We usually locate a few, and then they disappear, likely eaten by other bugs, within a day or two. This year, I decided to take matters into my own hands and nurture the caterpillars into butterflies. I had no clue it would turn into such a passion!

Monarch butterflies are in desperate need of human help. Their numbers have been steadily diminishing, falling by 80 percent in the last 20 years. The population is now much too small to be safe, which means that an early winter storm during their journey might wipe off the whole species. The condition of the honeybee may be more recognizable to you, but as a fellow pollinator, the monarch has also suffered as a consequence of environmental change, pesticide usage, and habitat loss. So, what can you do to guarantee that monarchs survive for future generations?

Raise Your Own Monarch Butterflies

CHAPTER ONE

WHY SHOULD WE RAISE BUTTERFLIES, MONARCH BUTTERFLIES, AND OTHER SPECIES?

We have the ability to rescue them from predation.

Wasps, birds, spiders, predatory stink and assassin bugs, ants, and a variety of other creatures prey on them from egg to adult. Predation isn't about survival of the fittest from egg to chrysalis. Eggs, caterpillars, and chrysalises are unable to flee. This is about rescuing many who might otherwise perish.

We have the ability to rescue them from sickness.

Nature is rife with disease. When we bring in eggs and caterpillars, we can prevent many of them from getting unwell, from minor bacterial infections to terrifying viruses like Nuclear Polyhedrosis Virus. Many lives are saved by raising butterflies in a hygienic environment with clean sanitary standards.

We can protect them against parasites such as OE

A protozoa that parasitize Monarch and Queen Butterflies, as well as other butterfly species that eat milkweed. OE may be prevented by bringing in eggs and sanitizing them, as well as sanitizing the plants we feed them.

We have the ability to rescue them from parasitoids.

Tachinid flies, chalcid wasps, and other parasitoids deposit their eggs within or on caterpillars or fragile chrysalises. We can safeguard them by bringing them in before they get infected.

NOTE: Disease, parasites, parasitoids, and predation are all strategies used by nature to maintain the species alive as a whole.

When we nurture caterpillars and others see what we accomplish, it inspires others to do the same. This devotion makes people aware of butterflies, their adversaries, and their needs.

It instills in our children the importance of respecting and protecting butterflies and the environment.

Our children learn from us while we nurture caterpillars. They understand the significance of creating and conserving habitat for pollinators other than butterflies.

It informs us about the hazards of pesticides.

Many of us grew up in an era when pesticides were advocated considerably more than they are now. Pesticides were thought to be crop savers. We re-evaluate our pesticide usage after breeding butterflies and seeing the effects of pesticides firsthand. We either restrict the kind of pesticides we use or completely eliminate pesticide usage. We begin to educate others, including nurseries, and fewer pesticides are used on plants as a consequence.

Butterfly host and nectar plant seeds and plants are shared by people.

Many gardeners give out seed, with some asking for a self-addressed, stamped envelope. This increases the amount of pesticide-free butterfly plants cultivated for butterfly habitat.

It is a pleasurable hobby.

Others get interested in what we do because we plainly enjoy it. We can educate people about butterflies. As a consequence, the number of butterflies increases. More habitat is being created. Pesticides are being used less often. Even who gets our vote in government may be influenced by whether or not they choose to safeguard our environment.

CHAPTER TWO

WHERE TO LOOK FOR CATERPILLARS

Finding your own caterpillars may be a gratifying undertaking depending on the season, where you reside, and how much time you have. Look for caterpillars by looking for plants that are recognized host plants for local butterflies and moths. This information may be found in field guides. Caterpillars may be found in a variety of host plants, including:

BUTTERFLY SPECIES	HOST PLANT
Milkweed	Monarch butterfly plant
Spicebush	Spicebush Swallowtail
Paw-paw	Zebra swallowtail
Sweet Gum, Walnut	The Luna Moth
Parsley, Dill, Fennel	Black Swallowtail
Cherry	Cecropia Moth, Viceroy, Red-Spotted Purple

If you don't have time or if the season isn't right for caterpillar hunting, there are a few firms that sell caterpillars. Painted Lady caterpillars are very simple to raise since you can purchase a growth medium for them, eliminating the need to obtain new host plant leaves every day. However, there are several disadvantages to growing caterpillars in this manner. A youngster, in particular, does not receive the full benefit of knowing how vital it is for caterpillars to consume the right host plant. Nonetheless, growing Painted Ladies on growth medium is a gratifying experience that is less reliant on the season outdoors and the leaves available.

Monarch Watch, a non-profit organization, sells butterfly larva of the well-known Monarch butterfly (www dot MonarchWatch dot org). Because of their vibrant colors and the popularity of the Monarch butterfly, these caterpillars are popular in many schools. The sole disadvantage to growing Monarch caterpillars is the need to locate their host plant, milkweed. Milkweed is both a popular garden plant and a prevalent weed. Several attractive types of milkweed are sold by many youngsters.

If you are fortunate enough to come across an adult female Saturniid moth, such as a Luna, Cecropia, or Polyphemus Moth, you may often

persuade her to lay eggs The majority of wild-caught females have already mated (unless they have JUST emerged). Because female moths are less particular about where they lay their eggs than certain butterflies, you may simply put the female in a big paper bag and fold it over to shut it firmly. Allow her to stay in there for a few days.

When you open the bag again, you're likely to discover eggs on the surface. Remove the eggs gently from the bag (or cut off the portion of the sack where the eggs were deposited) and put them in a small container. Mist the container gently on a regular basis to slightly raise the humidity. Maintain vigilance over your eggs! Before the eggs hatch, you must decide which host plants they will consume and find a handy supply of that host plant. Caterpillars may hatch in as little as three days. As soon as the caterpillar's hatch, they will need new host plants. A few leaves in the container (changed daily) will enough for your caterpillars until they start developing and consuming more.

INCLUDE HOST PLANTS

A host plant is a plant that a butterfly will deposit its eggs on. When the butterfly eggs hatch, the host plant provides food and protection to the developing caterpillars.

Plant a mixture of host and nectar plants to organically attract a diverse range of butterflies to your yard (butterflies are most attracted to pink, purple, yellow, and red flowers). Some of our favorite butterflies and their favored host plants are listed below:

- Queen Anne's lace, parsley, carrot, dill, fennel, and rue — Black Swallowtail Butterflies
- Monarch Butterflies — milkweed and butterfly weed.
- Thistle — Painted Lady Butterflies
- Rue's — Giant Swallowtail Butterflies
- Tiger Swallowtail Butterflies — Trees such as tulip, cherry, birch, and willow.
- Spicebush Swallowtail Butterflies — Sassafras and spicebush trees
- White Admiral Butterflies — Trees such as willow, aspen, poplar, and birch.

Tip: Avoid spraying pesticide or fertilizer on butterfly host and nectar plants. Organic farming is the most beneficial to butterflies! It's also critical to ensure that any plants you buy haven't been treated.

CHAPTER THREE

COLLECTION OF CATERPILLARS

Curly Parsley with a Black Swallowtail Butterfly Egg

If your host plants are doing well, it won't be long until butterflies notice them!

Every spring, my children and I plant a large amount of curly parsley in our butterfly garden and clay pots on our porch for black swallowtail butterflies. The parsley plants are covered with tiny black swallowtail caterpillars by late July!

In our butterfly garden, we also cultivate swamp milkweed for monarch butterflies. Finding monarch caterpillars is such a treat! The smallest caterpillars are about the size of a grain of rice, and they are even smaller when they are newborns.

Larvae of the Monarch Butterfly on Swamp Milkweed

Caterpillars are collected by carefully pinching off the leaf they are on. We never handle the caterpillars since they are so delicate.

If your caterpillar falls to the ground, gently pick it up with a leaf or a clean paintbrush—the caterpillar's feet will clasp the paintbrush's hair.

CHAPTER FOUR

MAKE A CATERPILLAR HOUSING

Making a caterpillar home is simple and enjoyable! In a 10-gallon aquarium with a screen terrarium cover, we love growing monarch and black swallowtail butterflies.

Caterpillar Habitat in a 10-Gallon Aquarium

We also have a mesh pop-up butterfly habitat, but because we keep our caterpillars outdoors, I prefer the tank or screen cage.

Black Swallowtail Caterpillars in a Mesh Pop-Up Butterfly Habitat

I do, however, often utilize the pop-up habitat for tiny newborn monarch caterpillars. When they become too large to fit through the screen, I relocate them to the aquarium or a Nano ReptiBreeze.

I don't put dirt in the mesh habitat or the Repti-Breeze, but I do cover the bottom with soft felt. The felt makes the homes simple to clean and provides something for the caterpillars' feet to grab onto if they fall.

Raise Your Own Monarch Butterflies

1. Fill the bottom of a clean aquarium with a 1-inch layer of dry garden soil. I like to imagine that the dirt mimics the natural environment of the caterpillars in our butterfly garden or potted plants. The soil also aids in the breakdown of caterpillar frass (droppings), so keeping the environment clean.

If you don't want to use dirt, cover the aquarium's bottom with a layer of paper towel or felt. Make it a point to alter it every day!

2. Inside the habitat, place a tiny potted plant or a water-filled mason jar with a frog top. The frog lid should be tightly packed with the caterpillar's host plant stems. You certainly don't want any caterpillars to go into the water!

If you can't compress the stems tightly enough, try putting cheesecloth or parchment paper beneath the frog cover and punching little holes for your plants to access the water.

In addition, we prefer to make sure the host plant is in contact with the aquarium walls. That way, if any caterpillars fall off and start wandering, they can simply find their way back home.

3. Fill the aquarium with a few thin sticks. Monarch caterpillars nearly usually climb to the screen to develop a chrysalis, in our experience. On the glass walls, the sticks, and the screen, black swallowtail caterpillars will produce chrysalids.

Larvae of the Black Swallowtail in Caterpillar Habitat

4. Place your caterpillar housing in a shaded spot outdoors. When the weather is hot and dry, spray the plants lightly with

distilled water. Simply cover the aquarium with a small plastic container if it rains.

Black Swallowtail Caterpillars in their Infancy

Tip: I put very few young caterpillars in a "caterpillar nursery," which is just a plastic food container! I put the package into the aquarium's corner. When it's time to replace the plants, the caterpillar nursery makes it simple to keep track of the tiny fellas.

A Few More Pointers:

1) Be prepared for a lot of phrasing (poop). They are tiny, roundish, dark green/black in color, and do not stink; yet, they are abundant. If your caterpillars are contained, you will need to clean them out on a regular basis. If the caterpillars are out in the open, you should place something down to collect the grass.

2) Before pupating, many caterpillars will empty their digestive systems. This is a greenish liquid, so depending on what surface your caterpillars are on, you may want to cover it with paper towels or newspaper.

4) Avoid placing your caterpillars'/chrysalises' housing in direct sunlight. Caterpillars may get overheated, and chrysalises may dry out. Having said that, we have grown caterpillars in front of a sunny window with the shade half-open. We didn't have an issue since they were "open" caterpillar houses. I believe an enclosed caterpillar home in the sun would be much too hot. To be on the safe side, keep your caterpillars away from direct sunlight.

CHAPTER FIVE

WHAT DO CATERPILLARS EAT?

Caterpillars, which are the larvae of butterflies and moths, eat virtually entirely vegetation. Most caterpillars will gladly eat on leaves, while others may dine on other plant components such as seeds or flowers.

Specialist Feeders vs. Generalist Feeders

Herbivorous caterpillars are classified as either generalist feeders or specialized feeders. **Generalist caterpillars** eat a wide range of plants. Willow, elm, aspen, paper birch, cottonwood, and hackberry caterpillars, for example, eat willow, elm, aspen, paper birch, cottonwood, and hackberry. Caterpillars of the **black swallowtail** will eat any member of the parsley family, including parsley, fennel, carrot, dill, and even Queen Anne's lace. Specialist caterpillars eat only on limited, related groupings of plants. **The monarch caterpillar** solely eats the leaves of milkweed plants.

A few caterpillars are carnivorous, preying on tiny, soft-bodied insects such as aphids. A peculiar moth larva (Ceratophaga vicinella) found in the southern United States feeds only on the shells of deceased gopher tortoises. Tortoiseshells are comprised of keratin, which most scavengers find difficult to digest.

Making a Decision on What to Feed Your Caterpillar

If you're planning to keep a caterpillar in captivity, you'll need to discover its dietary preferences, whether it specialized in a certain species of plant or eats on a range of host plants. You can't expect a caterpillar to adjust to eating anything other than its typical diet if you put it in a container containing grass.

So, if you don't know what sort of caterpillar it is, how do you know what to feed it? Take a look around the area where you discovered it. Was it found on a plant? Collect some of the plant's leaf and feed it to it. Otherwise, collect samples of whatever plants are around and observe to see if it selects one.

Also, bear in mind that we often locate caterpillars when they migrate away from their host plants in search of a location to pupate. So, if the caterpillar you picked up was crossing a pavement or plodding through your yard when you picked it up, it may not have been hungry at all.

The (Nearly) Universal Caterpillar Food: Oak Leaves

If your caterpillar refuses to eat anything you've given it, try gathering some oak leaves. There are well over 500 moth and butterfly species that feed on oak leaves, so the chances are in your favor if you try Quercus leaves. Many caterpillars also like the foliage of cherry, willow, or apple trees. When everything else fails, try the leaves of one of the most potent perennials for caterpillars.

Plants Caterpillar-Eat in Your Garden

More than nectar plants are required to create a genuine butterfly garden. Caterpillars, too, need nourishment! Include caterpillar host plants, and you'll attract a lot more butterflies when they come to deposit eggs on your plants.

Include some caterpillar host plants from this list while designing your butterfly garden. A properly designed butterfly garden benefits not just this year's butterflies, but future generations as well!

Common Garden Butterflies and Their Host Plants

Butterfly	Caterpillar Host Plants
American painted lady	Pearly Everlasting
black swallowtail	dill, fennel, carrot, parsley
cabbage whites	mustards
checkered whites	mustards
common buckeye	snapdragons, monkey flowers
eastern comma	elm, willow, hackberry
emperors	hackberry
giant swallowtail	lime, lemon, hoptree, prickly ash
grass skippers	little bluestem, panic grass
greater fritillaries	violets
gulf fritillary	passion vines
heliconians	passion vines
monarch butterfly	milkweeds
mourning cloak	willow, birch
painted lady	thistles
palamedes swallowtail	red bay

pearl crescent	asters
pipevine swallowtail	pipevines
question mark	elm, willow, hackberry
red admiral	nettles
red spotted purple	cherry, poplar, birch
silver-spotted skipper	black locust, indigo

CHAPTER SIX

WAIT RIGHT NOW

That's right...now you just have to wait! The caterpillars will eat and eat and eat until they are tall and fat!

Continue to provide them with new plants and keep their environment clean. Check the tank for spiders, ants, and flying insects, and remove any that you discover.

Raise Your Own Monarch Butterflies

When the caterpillar is ready, it will cease feeding, hang upside down, and pupate into a chrysalis.

Pupa Monarch

LET THE BUTTERFLIES OUT!

It's always exciting to release butterflies and watch them fly for the first time! My boys applaud and follow them around the yard.

1. But when should butterflies be released after hatching? When a butterfly emerges from its cocoon, its wings are floppy and moist. Allow the butterfly's wings to dry for about 2 hours in the caterpillar home. The butterfly will be ready to fly after this time.

You might also feed the butterfly watermelon, orange slices, fresh nectar flowers, or a honey-water mix made up of 9 parts purified water and 1 part raw honey if preferred. Pour the honey water solution onto a clean paper towel, then set it on a plate or tiny plastic cover, such as a sour cream lid. (This is something we don't usually do because we normally release our butterflies as soon as they're ready to fly.)

2. Lift the tank lid gently. If the butterfly does not immediately fly away, have your youngster carefully slip a single finger between the butterfly's front legs. The butterfly will creep across their finger and then fly away!

3. If the butterfly does not fly away, take it to a garden and let it wander on a flower, or return it to its environment to dry.

Monarch Butterfly

Raise Your Own Monarch Butterflies

CHAPTER SEVEN

RAISING BUTTERFLY CATERPILLAR INDOORS

It is simple to raise butterfly caterpillars indoors. However, there are several pointers that might help your child-rearing success.

Move the vase/pot to the side if you are rearing caterpillars in a popup, aquarium, or another container and their food is not touching the bottom or edges of the container. If a caterpillar crawls off the plant to molt, it may have difficulty finding the leaves again if the leaves are not contacting the container's bottom, top, or sides. Take note of this image. The plant is not touching the popup's bottom or sides. Caterpillars might spend hours crawling around without locating milkweed. Move the plant to a location where it will contact the side of the popup. As it creeps about the area, a caterpillar will readily locate the plant.

Mosquitoes and ticks can be a problem when strolling in the woods or fields. Mosquito and tick-borne infections are no laughing matter and may be fatal. It is strongly advised to use a mosquito and tick repellent. **WASH YOUR HANDS THOROUGHLY BEFORE CONTACTING BUTTERFLIES, CHRYSALIS, OR CATERPILLAR!** They might not be affected by the repellant. However, depending on the type of repellant and the kind of butterfly or moth, it may harm them. The two major ideas are to a) protect oneself and to b) safeguard butterflies and caterpillars. The most important things to remember are to spray repellant

AWAY from any living bug or their plants and to properly wash your hands before touching anything alive or its food.

People who reside in the southern states or old houses frequently find it necessary to apply insect repellent. Ants, roaches, scorpions, and spiders are also attracted to our dwellings. If you must spray, make sure your insects are completely out of the house.

I just utilized an insect fogger in my laundry room to get rid of several moths in bird food. The laundry room was 35 feet away from the only caterpillar container I had in the home. It was not just 35 feet away, but it was in a completely distinct room, with a closed door and 35 feet separating the fogger and the caterpillars. I didn't even consider the ductwork for our air conditioner (which cut on as the fogger was filling the room with insecticide). We didn't see the popup was coated with dark green vomit from sick caterpillars until it was too late. They were all killed.

Disinfect any previous raising containers you utilized. Each caterpillar group should be placed in a sterilized or "fresh" rearing container. If you make a throw away, such as a shoebox, don't use it again for another batch of caterpillars. They have heinous illnesses! However, keep in mind that when you handle unhealthy caterpillars, you spread the germs to whatever you touch, even the bleach bottle handle. as well as the lid When disinfecting rearing containers, use a bleach wipe or something similar to clean down anything you may have touched, especially if you had sickness difficulties with your previous batch of caterpillars.

If a caterpillar appears to be in distress, either euthanize it or raise it separately from the rest of your caterpillars. Disease, like individuals, may be passed from one to another. Nature has a lot of unpleasant shocks in store for caterpillars. Nature only enables one or two people out of every hundred to reach adulthood. One of the reasons they die is due to disease.

Caterpillars develop cuticles that are too huge for them (skin). The caterpillar molts when its cuticle can no longer expand any further (crawls out of its cuticle). Leave your caterpillar alone if it is off the plant and sitting calmly. A caterpillar that isn't moving on its own should not be moved. Be mindful that certain species cannot complete their molting if they are transported. They will perish if they do not finish molting. When Monarch caterpillars are molting, they usually do well if they are transferred.

Keep in mind that touching a dog or cat with flea and tick treatment before ministering to your caterpillars might result in the death of your caterpillars. The monthly drug will remain in the skin oils of the dog or cat, and if you touch the creature, the drug (poison) will be on your hands. Always wash your hands thoroughly before feeding or touching your caterpillars' food. Protect your pets, but also your eggs, caterpillars, chrysalises, and adult butterflies.

Raise Your Own Monarch Butterflies

CHAPTER EIGHT

Building a Butterfly Garden

A butterfly garden is no more difficult to create than any other garden, and with a few basic guidelines, you can simply transform an existing garden area into a butterfly haven or start a new garden from scratch. Butterfly gardens can be as large or as little as you want them to be.

My fascination with butterflies began with a decorative container filled with parsley (among other things). We were taken aback when we discovered some lovely tiny caterpillars all over it one day. That sparked a lifelong interest in me, and over the next few years, I transformed all of my garden plants into butterfly nectar and host plants. I am still expanding the gardens and/or introducing more butterfly plants.

Butterfly Gardens Follow the Same Gardening Procedures As Well.

Soil preparation is similar to that of any other garden. Plants' specific requirements vary, but in general, most plants require good soil with a particular quantity of organic matter mixed throughout to thrive. Fortunately, butterflies and native plants go hand in hand, so you'll almost surely discover plants that grow well in your soil type while also being appealing to butterflies.

Because butterfly plants generally include a variety of native species, your fertilizer requirements may be reduced. Organic fertilizer is usually preferable, but I have had no issues with the usage of some chemical fertilizer in the soil.

Butterflies are unconcerned with the geometry of a garden, so you may design it whatever you want: garden plots, foundation plantings, along fences, and even containers.

Plant your taller plants at the rear, arrange plants with complementary colors if feasible, and aim to have a variety of flowers in bloom throughout the spring, summer, and fall. This is not only aesthetically beautiful, but your butterflies will love the various heights of the blooms as well as the availability of nectar during the butterfly season. Furthermore, a greater variety of plants/flowers correlates to a greater diversity of butterflies.

If at all feasible, design your butterfly garden with some wind protection in mind. Because I have butterfly plants all over my house, deck, and yard, certain spots are more protected than others. It's never been an issue for us, and unless you live in a place where it's continuously windy all summer, I wouldn't allow the absence of a windbreak to put you off. That being said, if you can include shelter in your design, it is fantastic. As a windbreak, plants like butterfly bushes (Buddleia davidii, a nectar source) or spice bushes (Lindera benzoin, a host plant) would be excellent.

Butterflies prefer a sunny garden.

Butterflies are cold-blooded and require warmth to fly. Many butterflies require temperatures of 65 degrees Fahrenheit or higher to fly, thus they use the sun to warm themselves. It's no surprise, however, that the majority of butterfly nectar plants are sun-loving plants.

There are more host plant kinds that will withstand some (or a lot) of shade. So, arrange your floral nectar plants for sunny regions, while some of the host plants will do well in part-shade or shaded regions. If you can locate at least 6 hours of direct sunshine in portions of your yard, your options for nectar plants (and host plants) will expand significantly.

If you reside in an extremely shady place, though, all is not lost. Some butterflies prefer shaded, woodland settings, and, unsurprisingly, these butterflies do not rely on flower nectar as their primary food source. Instead, they are drawn to rotten fruit, excrement, tree sap, and so on.

I have no experience with butterfly gardens in very shaded areas, but if that were the case, I would focus on planting shade-loving host plants (Dutchman's Pipevine, Lindera benzoin), using butterfly fruit feeders rather than nectar plants, and experimenting with a few shade-loving nectar plants such as Sweet Joe Pye Weed and Cut-leaf toothwort (Cardamine diphyllos) (Monarda fistulosa).

Plant Selection for Your Garden

Plants that are vital to butterflies fall into two categories: host plants and nectar plants. Essentially, nectar plants offer the nectar that adult butterflies consume from the blooms, whereas host plants give the leaves that caterpillars eat before transforming into chrysalises (from which the adult butterfly emerges). Passing butterflies will be drawn to nectar plants, while egg-laying female adult butterflies will be drawn to host plants

Having both results in colonies and bigger populations of butterflies that remain. It completes the butterfly life cycle and transforms a butterfly garden into a joyful and intriguing location.

When selecting plants, bear in mind that types local to your area will perform best in your soil/environment. Milkweed, for example, has many distinct types that are adapted to different parts of the United States, and Monarch butterflies will consume a large portion of the various variations. However, I do not limit myself to native species and am always willing to experiment with a new butterfly plant in my garden.

Try to get your plants from smaller garden stores, online wildlife/nature/organic-type nurseries, or grow them from seed. This is done to prevent the use of insecticides. Growing from seed is the most secure option, although many smaller nurseries can inform you whether or not their plants have been pesticide-treated.

I've heard of plants from big-box retailers harming caterpillars because they've been pesticide-treated. I'm thinking the nectar plants aren't sprayed with pesticides as frequently as the host plants are since the host plant producers need to keep the caterpillars away so they can sell some plants! So, be aware that plants purchased from large shops may be toxic, particularly to caterpillars, for a month or longer after purchase.

Group your plants to make it easier for butterflies to find your garden.

A butterfly garden is the ideal setting for dramatic color outbursts! With butterflies, more is more, and they like group plantings of the same plant (seeds are inexpensive if you don't mind growing plants from seed). For example, if you have a bag of Zinnia seeds, don't scatter them across your garden; instead, create a huge patch of zinnias. The same may be said for host plants. Plant clusters make it simpler for butterflies to see, smell, and so discover your garden.

Despite the fact that bigger is preferable, don't be discouraged if you only have a tiny room. As I indicated before, my butterfly obsession began with a parsley plant in a pot. So, whether it's a vast colorful garden plot or a few vivid pots, plant lavishly.

There are no pesticides in Butterfly Gardens

Pesticides are intended to kill insects, including butterflies and caterpillars. Using native plants can help limit the need for pesticides, and if you want to maintain the garden healthy for your butterflies and caterpillars, you may just have to tolerate the occasional bug. Every year, aphids and milkweed bugs attack my milkweed, yet neither prevents caterpillars from devouring it down to bare stalks. If a major problem arises, you may need to investigate various non-chemical solutions.

Raise Your Own Monarch Butterflies

CHAPTER NINE

CHOOSING THE IDEAL BUTTERFLY HOUSE

Life is like a butterfly. You may either chase it or let it come to you.

It is simple to attract butterflies with a little knowledge and patience. The fundamental stages in making your garden an appealing home for many kinds of butterflies include including butterfly host and nectar plants, decreasing and/or eliminating the use of pesticides, and providing water and shelter.

What exactly is a butterfly's safe haven? Butterflies seek for peaceful locations with tall plants and grasses to sleep in through the spring, summer, and early fall. Only in the late fall and winter months do these winged beauties seek additional protection. When the temperature drops, butterflies begin their yearly journey, overwinter in a cocoon or chrysalis, or hibernate as adults. A butterfly house may aid in the survival of butterfly species that spend the winter as adults, but in fact, they are more likely to utilize woodpiles and other natural nooks and crannies.

Butterfly homes, like birdhouses, come in a variety of shapes and sizes, ranging from a basic wooden box with a sloping roof to intricate architectural models of beach cottages, log cabins, cathedrals, and garden sheds. A butterfly house, as opposed to a birdhouse, features long, narrow slots rather than a spherical aperture. In principle, these slots enable butterflies to enter but keep birds out.

When searching for a butterfly home, opt for one with a back door that opens for simple cleaning. You should also include a piece of bark or a short branch inside for butterflies to perch on if they so want. If you are a do-it-yourselfer, you can find a variety of butterfly house plans on the Internet. Make careful you use untreated lumber, preferably pine or cypress.

Butterflies are drawn to bright colors such as pink, purple, red, and yellow. Consider painting your house in a Caribbean color scheme or covering it with large, bright flowers. To extend the life of your paint job, apply a clear coat.

Residents of the Butterfly House

Butterfly houses are charming in any setting and are frequently overlooked as garden ornaments. Unfortunately, this is true in the majority of cases. Coaxing butterflies to use the house necessitates knowing which species will use it and what habitat they require. During the winter, butterflies such as mourning cloaks, tortoiseshells, angel wings, and red admirals may seek safety in a butterfly house.

Landscaping and house placement

Place your butterfly house about four feet high on a post, fence, or tree in a wind-protected spot. Wind movement makes butterflies feel uneasy, so hanging the home where it could wobble is not a smart idea. The border of a woodland area is a great place since the trees give shelter while the open region allows nectar plants to grow.

Plants that serve as hosts should be planted nearby. The butterflies described previously use willow, elm, buckthorn, nettles, and hops as host plants. Plant nectar plants such as asters, milkweed, phlox, purple coneflower, and wild bergamot around the butterfly house.

A butterfly house adds a lovely touch to any landscape. We also offer information on how to make a butterfly garden if you need it. If you follow the guidelines, you could be surprised when these wonderful flying insects decide to make your home their home.

CHAPTER TEN

IS A BUTTERFLY AN INSECT?

Insects outnumber all other animals on the planet. By far and away! Currently, eight out of every ten creatures on the planet are insects or other Arthropods. We know of over a million distinct insect species and are constantly uncovering new ones.

So, what factors influence bug status? Here is a five-item checklist:

1. There is no backbone. The creature is literally devoid of a spine. Creatures are the only invertebrates that can fly.
2. The body is protected by a chitin exoskeleton, whereas other creatures get structure from an internal skeleton.
3. The body is split into three sections: the head, the thorax, and the abdomen.
4. On top of the head, a pair of antennae sit.
5. Three pairs of jointed legs connect to the body's thoracic region.

It's very clear that butterflies have all of the necessary characteristics of a real insect—until we come to the fifth item on the checklist. There is a huge group of butterflies (including several well-known species such as Monarchs, Emperors, Admirals, and Fritillaries) that appear to have just four legs. However, the essential word here is "appear."

Butterfly Specifications:

The Nymphalidae is a family of fliers that appear to have four legs. They have a pair of forelegs that are severely truncated and difficult to see. Some people preserve these essentially vestigial appendages against their thorax or coiled up towards their head. Why do they no longer walk with their legs?

What do they say to one another?

Scientists aren't sure, but one theory is that the insects utilize their smaller forelegs for communication and signaling rather than weight-bearing. The smaller legs are typically coated in fuzz, lending credence to the communication upgrade argument.

Butterflies have a fascinating and extraordinary history of adaptability. The caterpillar in its larval stage is a voracious eater with a fat physique. It gathers and stores the nutrients it will require for its next stage of development as a chrysalis. The chrysalis then develops into a beautiful, ethereal butterfly.

The caterpillar is just concerned with nutrition, whilst the butterfly is solely concerned with reproduction. Its brilliantly colored wings aid in attracting a partner of the same species. The newly developed proboscis enables it to consume the nectar required for flight fuel. The female butterfly explores a variety of plants in search of ideal nesting sites for her eggs.

What Characteristics Characterize a Great Butterfly Garden?

The best butterfly gardens provide food and room for all phases of the Lepidoptera life cycle. Host plants are places where eggs can be placed and caterpillars can eat (and eat, and eat!). Untouched areas for chrysalis development are beneficial. Of course, you'll need as many blooms as possible to meet the nectar demands of the adult butterflies. These are all essential components of your butterfly habitat.

That's all there is to it! The butterfly is, in fact, an insect. We at Joyful Butterfly take great pleasure in assisting you in the care of some of the most beautiful Arthropod species. We genuinely hope these amazing animals offer you the delight they have provided us!

HOW LONG DOES RAISING BUTTERFLIES TAKE?

This varies by species, but on average, it takes 15–30 days to produce a butterfly from an egg.

Black Swallowtail Butterfly, a new species, has been released.

WHAT IS THE BEST WAY TO CUT MILKWEED FOR CATERPILLARS?

To prevent wilting, cut washed milkweed at a 45-degree angle with sharp garden pruners. After cutting the milkweed stem, immerse it in warm water. Alternatively, you might cut the stem in a sink with running warm water.

After cutting the milkweed stem, place it in a tiny glass bottle or a mason jar with a frog top. Remember, we don't want any caterpillars to fall into the water, so add parchment paper or cheesecloth under the frog cover if your host plant stems aren't packed tightly enough.

If you have a lot of monarch caterpillars, keep the milkweed in flower tubes. Plastic to-go cups are a terrific alternative if you're in a hurry! Simply insert the milkweed stem into the straw hole.

Larva of the Black Swallowtail

A child's interest in nature and the great outdoors is often piqued by learning how to nurture butterflies. Take hold of your curiosity and go outside as a family to play, learn, and experience every day!

CHAPTER ELEVEN

Butterfly Fun Facts

We've compiled a list of unusual butterfly facts to share with you. Astound your friends! Have fun!

- Butterflies range in size from 1/8 inch to over 12 inches.

- Butterflies can see in three colors: red, green, and yellow.

- Some believe that when the black bands on the Wooly Bear caterpillar are broad, cold winter is on its way.

- The highest speed of a butterfly is 12 miles per hour. Some moths can fly at speeds of up to 25 miles per hour!

- Monarch butterflies travel around 2,000 miles from the Great Lakes to the Gulf of Mexico before returning to the north in the spring.

- Butterflies are unable to fly if their body temperature falls below 86 degrees.

- Butterflies are shown in Egyptian paintings from Thebes, which date back 3,500 years.

- Antarctica is the sole continent where no Lepidoptera have been discovered.

- There are over 24,000 different species of butterflies. Moths are considerably more numerous: over 140,000 species have been identified worldwide.

- The Brimstone butterfly (Gonepteryx rhamni) lives the longest of any adult butterfly, lasting 9-10 months.

- In Some Cases, Moth caterpillars (Psychidae) construct a casing around themselves that they carry with them at all times. It is constructed of silk and plant or soil fragments.

- Some Snout Moth (Pyralididae) caterpillars dwell in or on water plants.

- Females of several moth species lack wings and may only move by crawling.

- The Morgan's Sphinx Moth of Madagascar has a proboscis (tube mouth) 12 to 14 inches long that it uses to extract nectar from the bottom of a 12-inch deep orchid found by Charles Darwin.

- Because they lack mouths, some moths never eat as adults. They must rely on the energy they accumulated as caterpillars to survive.
- Many butterflies can taste with their feet to determine whether the leaf they are sitting on is suitable for laying eggs on and providing nourishment for their larvae.

- One tropical rain forest tree contains more bug species than the whole state of Vermont.

- W.G. Bruce, an entomologist, presented a list of Arthropod references in the Bible in 1958. The Bible's most often named bugs are locust (24), moth (11), grasshopper (10), scorpion (10), caterpillar (9), and the bee (4).

- People consume insects, which is known as "Entomophagy" (people eating bugs). This practice has been done for ages in Africa, Australia, Asia, the Middle East, and North, Central, and South America. Why is this so? Because many bugs are high in protein and high in vitamins, minerals, and lipids.

- Many insects have the ability to carry 50 times their own body weight. This would be equivalent to an adult carrying two big vehicles full of passengers.

- There are over a million bug species described. Some estimate that there are between 15 and 30 million species.

- Most insects are valuable to humans because they consume other insects, pollinate crops, provide food for other animals, produce goods we need (such as honey and silk), or have medicinal properties.
- The exoskeleton, or skeleton, of butterflies and insects is located on the exterior of their bodies. This shields the insect and preserves water inside their bodies, preventing them from drying out.

CONCLUSION

Finally, if we want to ensure the future of migratory monarch populations, we must promote longer-term solutions, such as protecting and restoring habitat and addressing climate change."

So there you have it. To preserve migrating monarchs — and any wild creature — we need to do the hard work of creating and preserving habitat and pushing for legislation or whatever is needed to limit the effects of climate change.

Printed in the USA
CPSIA information can be obtained
at www.ICGtesting.com
LVHW021038180923
758512LV00010B/400